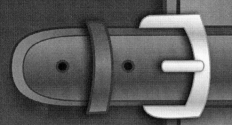

Briefcase Three:
Assessment Tools
for Inclusion
for Middle and High School

June Stride, Ed.D.

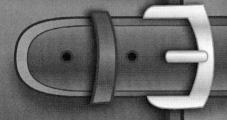

IEP
RESOURCES

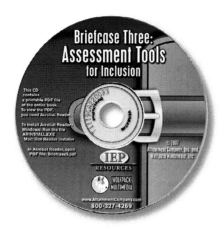

Win/Mac CD

The CD contains a printable PDF of this entire book. You can review and print pages from your computer. The PDF (Portable Document Format) file requires Acrobat Reader software.

If you have Acrobat Reader already installed on your computer, open the file BRIEFCASE3.pdf from the CD.

To install Acrobat Reader:
Windows: Run ARINSTALL.EXE on the CD
Mac: Run Reader Installer on the CD

After installation, run Acrobat Reader and open the file BRIEFCASE3.pdf from the CD.

Briefcase Three: Assessment Tools for Inclusion for Middle and High School

Author: June Stride, Ed. D.

Editors: Richard Wolfsdorf, Tom Kinney

Graphic Design/Illustration: Michael Mastermaker and Beverly Potts

ISBN: 1-57861-611-5

© 2007 Attainment Company, Inc. and Wolfpack Multimedia, Inc.

Printed in the United States of America

Attainment Company, Inc.
~~P.O. Box 930160~~

Distributed By:
Program Development Associates
5620 Business Ave. Suite B
Cicero, NY 13039
www.disabilitytraining.com
1-800-543-2119

Briefcase Three: Assessment Tools for Inclusion
for Middle and High School

TABLE OF CONTENTS

Dear Fellow Teachers,

Briefcase Three: Assessment Tools for Inclusion for Middle and High School *was developed to reduce the burden of these important responsibilities for the inclusion teachers. Herein you will find hints to prepare for assessment of students, self, the collaboration effort, curriculum and your inclusion program. To my mind, inclusion teaching necessitates collaborative work to include collaborative assessment involving not only coteachers but also, importantly, students.*

For your convenience, Briefcase Three has a special feature: a 'Student Brief.' The 'Student Brief' is designed as a stand-alone tool to encourage student involvement and responsibility for academic growth.

Moreover, Briefcase Three has tools and strategies to help you take your students from where they are now to where they need to be when they leave your class. Acknowledging their talents and skills or deficits helps you as well as your students, to develop and effectively maximize academic programs and instructional strategies.

Don't let assessment frighten you! Help lies ahead! Briefcase Three will give you TIPS and pointers for student preparation for testing and for inclusion grading, for assessment and evaluation. Briefcase Three will help make your inclusion journey more worthwhile, pleasant and academically productive.

Respectfully,
June Stride Ed. D.

HELPING STUDENTS PREPARE FOR ACADEMIC SUCCESS AND ASSESSMENT

1

Dear Teachers,

Why not take advantage of student energy and their growing desire for independence? Utilize 'free' minutes at the beginning or end of the period, especially at the beginning of the year, to engage them in a growth challenge.

The 'Student Brief' that follows can be the vehicle to start them on the path. Use the forms to allow them to determine their own strengths and weaknesses. Invite them to collaborate with you on their path to personal academic and behavioral growth.

When students feel involved and committed, discipline problems decline. As they channel their efforts in a directed positive manner, you'll be pleasantly surprised and pleased with the results!

Sincerely,
June

Helping Students Prepare for Academic Success and Assessment

ACADEMIC SUCCESS AND ASSESSMENT

Developing a study spot. Knowing your 'rights'

The Right Spot + the Right Time + the Right Equipment + the Right Habits = The Right Attitude.

Knowing your score...
personal learning strengths and weaknesses

Athletes and scholars who are honest in their personal learning assessment can use their knowledge to overcome weaknesses.

Succeeding academically:
'The Big 12 Rule Book for Academic Success'

Positive performance develops from positive behaviors. Here are 12 TIPS for growth toward academic success.

Check It Out!
Your Personal Student Communication Survey

Many students are quite unaware of the quality of their communication skills with adults and peers as well as the relationship to success.

Students who feel responsible for and are involved in their own academic growth and progress tend to work harder and want to work 'smarter.'

Making the grades: 12 study skills tips

Learn to study for success. Grades can be improved. Scores on tests can go up.

Reaching the top: Taking 'high stakes' tests

Test day strategies help. You can reduce test-taking stress and improve test results by following these simple hints on test day.

Your choice: Doing better on multiple choice type tests

Multiple choice answering can be tricky. Here are tools to help you select the best answer from the choices given.

Just write it: Succeeding on tests with written responses

Pointers to help you make the maximum points on essay or written response tests.

STUDENT BRIEF

SUCCESS IN SCHOOL

YOUR PLAYING FIELD
(study spot)

- Quiet
- Private while you are working
- Enough space to keep your supplies
- Enough space to spread out your stuff

Your equipment:

- **Flat surface of a desk or table:** Large enough to spread out your stuff. (Computer tables usually are not big enough to do anything other than computer work.)

- **Lamp or light.**

- **Comfortable chair:** Appropriate size for you and to reach the table.

- **Clock:** To monitor study and homework time and your breaks.

- **Calculator:** Plain or scientific, depending upon your teacher's request.

- **Pencil sharpener:** Keep the pencils sharp.

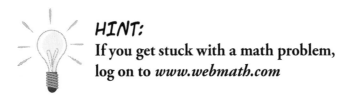

HINT:
If you get stuck with a math problem, log on to *www.webmath.com*

- **Writing and drawing tools:** Pencils, pens, colored markers, highlighters, glue, rulers, notebooks, lined paper, scissors, ruler, protractor, folders. Smaller storage box for these items: Pick one to fit neatly into larger storage box for all supplies.

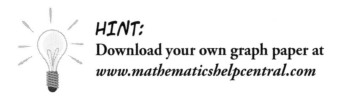

HINT:
Download your own graph paper at *www.mathematicshelpcentral.com*

- **Storage box large enough to hold all supplies:** A box on wheels is handy to roll your stuff away after use. Any kind of large shipping box will do!

- **Bonus:** Computer. For word processing of homework and reports, an older and slower computer works well.

HINT:
Use the family computer or one at your local libarary for Internet access to do research.

WHAT'S YOUR SCORE?

Athletes and scholars both need to know their learning strengths and weaknesses. What are yours?

 Check It Off!

 Check It Off!

Easy	Difficult	
		Speaking up in class, participating in discussions
		Volunteering answers
		Reading out loud
		Finding the main ideas
		Outlining
		Keeping an organized notebook
		Taking notes or copying notes accurately
		Mathematical computation
		Graphing
		Studying for tests
		Remembering facts
		Taking tests
		Searching on the Internet

Easy	Difficult	
		Working independently
		Staying on task, completing work
		Working with a partner or in a small group
		Writing complete sentences or paragraphs
		Staying focused
		Remembering material presented orally
		Recalling information you have read
		Making an oral presentation
		Learning from demonstrations
		Doing independent research
		Using appropriate language
		Reading and recalling subject area vocabulary
		Using computer software programs to enhance work

Total Easy = _____   **Total Difficult = _____**

Two important things I realize from completing this survey:

1. _____

_____

_____

2. _____

_____

_____

THE BIG 12: RULE BOOK FOR ACADEMIC SUCCESS

1. Show interest. Listen carefully in class.

2. Take neat and accurate notes or arrange to get copies from someone who does!

3. Prepare daily. Reread your notes each evening; reread notes before class.

4. Simplify study time. Keep neat, organized notebooks.

5. Copy homework assignments into an assignment pad or e-tablet.

6. Study daily at the same time in the same quiet location.

7. Bring required supplies to class daily.

8. Hand in assignments on time.

9. Participate. Ask questions to clarify.

10. Volunteer. Ask questions and ask when you need help.

11. Show motivation. Attend extra help sessions.

12. Use online homework assistance as needed.

YOUR PERSONAL COMMUNICATION SURVEY

1= Disagree   2 = Not sure   3 = Agree

1	2	3	
			I respect people who talk to me by looking at and listening to them.
			When someone talks to me, I stop what I'm doing to focus on what he/she is saying.
			People listen to me and show me respect.
			I can read and understand non-verbal/body language.
			If someone is rude to me, I control my temper.
			I do not make unkind remarks to or about people.
			I do not get into fights.
			I can express disagreement or anger without losing control.
			I do not pick on people, hit them or provoke them.
			If necessary, I ask an adult for help in handling a situation that is getting out of control.
			I can find safe locations within my school and/or community.
			I respect other peoples' property.
			I know a responsible person I can ask to help me stay out of trouble.
			I am able to steer clear of involvement in violence and weapon use.
			I stay on task and participate purposefully in group activities.
			I show value for other peoples' feelings and opinions.

I need to improve in the following communications areas:

_____

_____

_____

Other strengths or difficulties that I have:

_____

_____

_____

How Do You Rate?	
43-48 Excellent Skills	**26-35 Fair**
36-42 Good	**16-25 Danger Zone**

Study TIPS for Before or During Class

Rules of the Game

1. Organize your notebook into sections. Always date your notes and put them in order either in the front or back of the section.

2. Listen carefully during class. Ask questions any time you don't understand something.

3. Take complete notes. Keep study guides or dittos handed out by your teachers. If you are absent, get and copy the notes from a good student or from the teacher.

4. Spend the first moments of each class reviewing previous notes. Develop a dailty habit of rereading your notes from class.

5. Jot down new vocabulary words and terms. Keep a special section with subject area terms. Include meanings. Make flashcards for vocabulary words and/or main concepts. Study them whenever you have a few free minutes on the school bus, in waiting rooms, etc.

PRE-GAME PLANNING

STUDY TIPS FOR HOME OR DURING STUDY TIME... GETTING FIT

1. Try to study at the same time and in the same quiet place every day.

2. Plan ahead. Set aside time over the weekend to review the week's notes, vocabulary and main concepts.

3. Use a highlighter. Highlight only the MOST important information.

4. During study time before an exam, make a checklist of important things you should know. Cross them off the list as you study them.

5. Get in the habit of jotting down questions you want answered by your teacher. Write down questions you think might be on a test; be sure you can answer them.

STUDY TIPS FOR TEXTBOOK ASSIGNMENTS

- Pre-read textbook readings by scanning the assignment.

- Look at the pictures and read the captions.

- Use a 3 x 5 card held directly below your reading place to focus attention on the selected passage.

- Look at all the topic headings.

- Start by focusing on prepared questions at the end of the assignment.

- Ask yourself "What is this chapter trying to say?"

- Read the chapter with a questioning mind looking for who, what, when, where, why, how.

- Reread and try to summarize the main topics in your own words.

- Make flash cards or take notes on new vocabulary and important concepts.

WHAT ABOUT A STUDY BUDDY?

- Think carefully before deciding on a study buddy.

- If you decide to get a study buddy, select someone serious about learning.

- Set a time period for study and stick to it.

- Determine specifically what you intend to do.

- Do not waste time. Do not talk about other non-study topics.

- Work together on a regular basis to review notes, vocabulary, concepts, worksheets.

- If you find that it is not productive, discontinue and study on your own or look for a more effective study buddy match.

REACHING THE TOP: 10 TIPS FOR HIGH STAKES TESTS

1. To reduce stress and anxiety, do not talk to others about the test on the day of the test.

2. Clear your desk except for the required tools (pen, pencil, highlighter, ruler, calculator, etc.)

3. Listen carefully to instructions. Read instructions carefully to yourself.

4. Highlight what you must do to answer the question.

5. Highlight choices or vocabulary terms that appear in test questions that can help you in your answer.

6. Note how much time you have. Scan the test format and the point structure for each section. Decide how you can best use your time to get the most points.

7. Before you begin, write down any memorized study hints, formulas, and facts in the margins so you don't forget them.

8. Look through the test and highlight terms or ideas that might help you.

9. Do not spend time on a question about which you are unsure, circle it or make a notation in the margin. Return to it. You may recognize the answer in another question.

10. After you have finished, go back over the entire test to make sure that you have answered every question.

TIPS FOR EXAM SUCCESS

Multiple Choice Type Tests

- If two answers are similar, pick the one that you feel is best. Avoid answers with phrases including always, never.

- Select an answer that uses grammar correctly.

- Place answers in the correct location on "bubble sheets" or answer sheets.

- Read the question and answer it in your own words before looking at the choices. Find the answer that corresponds.

- If you have to guess from a wide range of numbers, pick one in the middle.

- Try to eliminate two choices. Select the best remaining answer.

TESTS WITH WRITTEN RESPONSES

- Highlight or underline exactly what is asked of you. If there are several parts to the question, number them so you answer all parts.

- Highlight verbs that tell what you are to do. If you are to compare items, do not list; if you are to describe, do not compare, etc.

- Make a brief outline before beginning to write your answer in sentence form.

- Make certain you give key concepts and enough information to answer the question.

- Get to the point. Consider using the wording of the question in your answer.

Dear Teachers,

Teaching an inclusion class of diverse learners is a challenge. Sharing that responsibility and learning to teach collaboratively is another challenge. One thing is certain, diverse learners need diversity not only in instruction, materials and strategies but also for assessment.

This next section of Briefcase Three is full of TIPS to help you collaboratively determine the how, what, when, and why of assessment. Let these suggestions guide you and your co-teacher in making assessment fair, worthwhile and valid.

Sincerely,

June

TIPS for Teachers... About Assessment

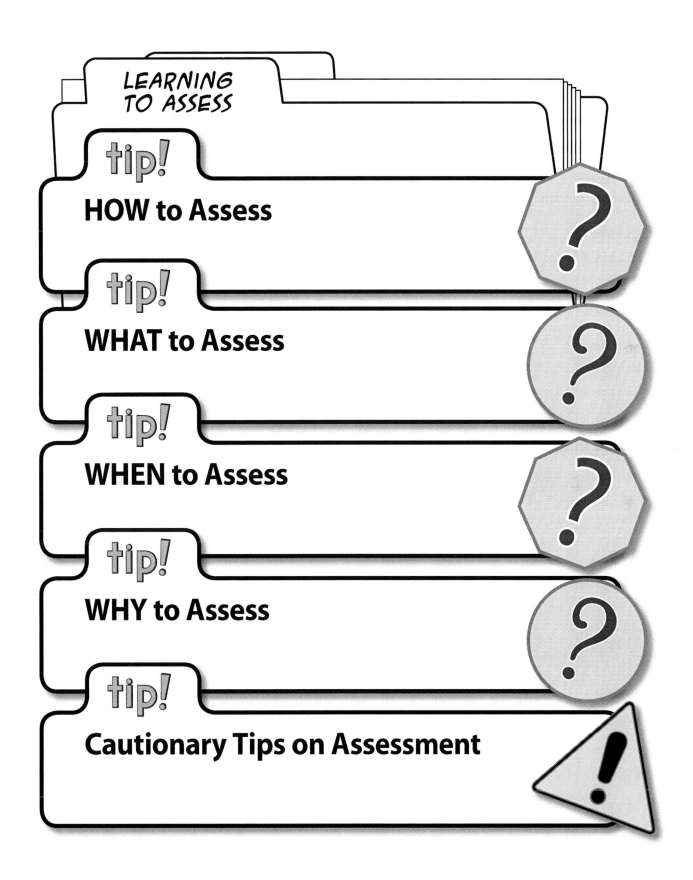

LEARNING TO ASSESS

tip!
HOW to Assess

tip!
WHAT to Assess

tip!
WHEN to Assess

tip!
WHY to Assess

tip!
Cautionary Tips on Assessment

TIPS FOR EXAM SUCCESS

Things to Do!

Know HOW to Assess

- Use IEP mandated testing modifications.
- Review IEP goal achievement.
- Use multiple assessment strategies.
- Analyze your grading policy to accurately reflect student process, product and progress.
- Analyze your grading policy to determine if it conveys the desired message about performance to students and parents.
- Explain your methods and purposes of assessment to students.
- Assess informally by watching and listening.
- Assess formally in preparation for 'high stakes' tests.

Know WHAT to Assess

- Curriculum you have taught.
- Curriculum aligned with state standards.
- Extent of mastery of content/curricular objectives.
- Extent of mastery of behavioral goals.

Know WHEN to Assess

- Assess often to provide multiple opportunities for students to demonstrate mastery.

- Assess daily (informally) to monitor your effectiveness.

- Assess regularly to plan for remediation.

Know WHY to Assess

- Determine level at which students are performing.

- Be a guide for student placement.

- Use as a learning tool and for determining the need for re-teaching.

- Determine your collaborative proficiency.

- Provide opportunities for re-assessment to promote learning.

- Determine need to modify your teaching pace, practices and strategies.

- Determine instructional effectiveness.

- Determine collaborative teaching effectiveness.

- Determine how and in what ways some students were successful and others not.

ASSESSMENT TIPS FOR TEACHERS

Assessment Cautions

- Do not forget IEP testing modifications.

- Do not 'borrow a co-teacher's exams to assess your students' progress in your class.

- Do not confuse assessment with grading.

- Do not use assessment as a 'gotcha' for students.

- Do not over *assess*.

- Do not use a solitary assessment tool to determine progress.

- Do not use a solitary assessment tool to determine a report card grade.

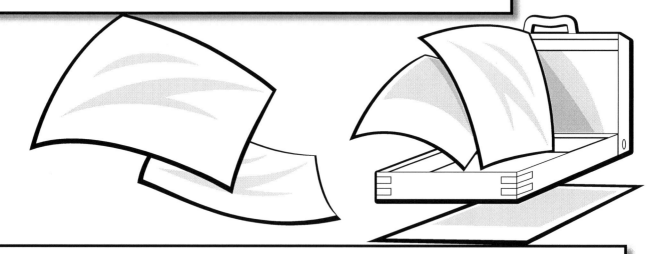

More Assessment Cautions

- Do not assume that students and parents will automatically understand the purpose for assessment.

- Do not assume that students and parents will automatically understand your assessment style and format.

- Do not limit assessment to students. Assess yourself, your collaborative efforts and your program.

- Do not be afraid to respond openly to questions about how, why, and in what ways you have assessed.

- Do not use assessment tools that have no content validity for your class.

- Do not teach with assessment results as the primary underlying purpose.

Dear Teachers,

Rubrics? What are they and why do educators hear so much about them? Of what value are they, especially to the inclusion teacher(s)? And, if they are important and helpful, why haven't we been shown how to make them and to use them effectively?

If these are questions you have asked yourself, the following section has been designed with you in mind. Starting with descriptions, going on to purposes, following with instructions and concluding with samples, this section tells you everything you need to know about rubrics. Importantly, it also shows you how and why to get started using them to make your assessments more objective and meaningful.

Sincerely,

June

Using Rubrics

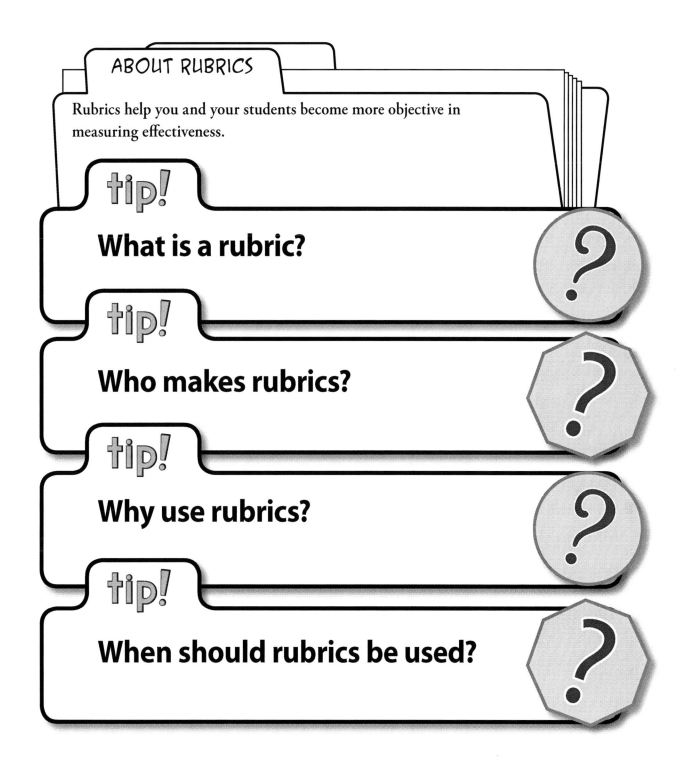

ABOUT RUBRICS

Rubrics help you and your students become more objective in measuring effectiveness.

tip!

What is a rubric?

tip!

Who makes rubrics?

tip!

Why use rubrics?

tip!

When should rubrics be used?

USING RUBRICS TO ASSESS

What is a Rubric?

- A rating scale.

- A set of standards used to evaluate content, process or products.

Who Makes Rubrics?

- Teachers: while focused on lesson planning.

- Teachers: to assess learning in a meaningful manner.

- Teachers: to determine mastery of given content, process or product.

- Students: for direct involvement in learning.

- Students: to focus understanding of academic expectations and assessment.

Why Use Rubrics?

- Use to gain powerful information about learning.

- Use to help adjust instruction.

- Use to determine the extent of individual or class proficiency on given topic or process.

- Use to determine teacher proficiency in reaching objectives.

- Use to determine how it is necessary to change teaching in order to improve student performance.

- Use to reduce the subjectivity of assessment.

- Use to focus teaching instruction and attention on major objectives.

- Use to allow students to understand expectations.

- Use to allow students to understand the outcome of assessment.

When Should Rubrics Be Used?

- Use *BEFORE* starting work on a product or process, to clarify criteria for students.

- Use *BEFORE* starting work on content, product or process, to clarify criteria for teachers in determining desired outcomes.

- Use for alternative assessments.

- Use to help teachers more objectively determine grades.

- Use to help teachers assess students with diverse abilities /talents/ disabilities.

- Use to allow for objective multi-modal assessment.

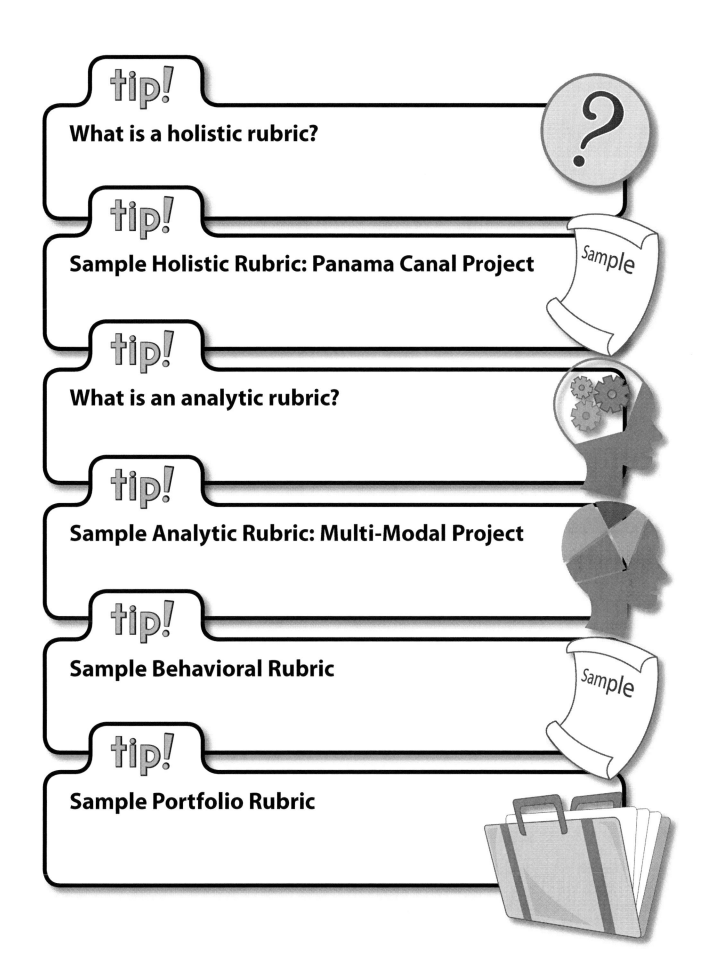

tip!

What is a holistic rubric?

tip!

Sample Holistic Rubric: Panama Canal Project

Sample

tip!

What is an analytic rubric?

tip!

Sample Analytic Rubric: Multi-Modal Project

tip!

Sample Behavioral Rubric

Sample

tip!

Sample Portfolio Rubric

HOLISTIC RUBRICS

Holistic Rubric

- A rating scale that considers the whole, the content, the project or the process with a set of specific criteria to determine the extent to which expectations have been met.

- A rating scale that is easy to construct and use but normally does not yield as much feedback as an analytic rubric.

HOLISTIC RUBRIC: PANAMA CANAL PROJECT

Score	Description	Student self-assessment	Teacher Assessment	Grade
5	Drawings of the Panama Canal area. Shows bodies of water to include depths; uses a series of pictures to demonstrate ship passage through the canal: before entry, during and after ship's exit. Drawings are neat and attractively presented. All parts included, a clear and complete understanding is demonstrated.			**A**
4	Clearly labels the major bodies of water involved to include depths. Labeled parts of the canal involved in passage of ships. Drawings are neat. Key parts are included, demonstrates understanding.			**B**
3	Labels major bodies of water. Labels the canal. Locks are not shown or labeled; depths of water are not included. Some key parts are missing, demonstrates partial understanding.			**C**
2	Labels the area. The locks and major bodies of water are not shown or correctly labeled. Many key parts are missing, understanding is minimal.			**C-**
1	Did not demonstrate understanding of the project.			(Unsatisfactory) **D**
0	Did not attempt project.			(Unsatisfactory) **F**

Comments:

_____

_____

_____

_____

_____

_____

HOLISTIC RUBRIC

Score	Description	Student self-assessment	Teacher Assessment	Grade
5				A
4				B
3				C
2				C-
1				(Unsatisfactory) D
0				(Unsatisfactory) F

Comments:

_____

_____

_____

_____

_____

_____

ANALYTIC RUBRIC FOR A MULTI-MODAL PROJECT

Criteria	0	Beginning 1	Progressing 2	Proficient 3	Superior 4	Student assess-	Teacher assess-
Visual aspect	No drawing attempted.	Graphic poorly done, incomplete, not accurate and not labeled.	Basic graphic, not completely labeled, parts left out.	Graphic neatly done and included required information. Parts were labeled.	Graphic accurate and detailed. Labeling explained functions of parts. Colors were used for differentiation.		
Oral aspect	Refused to present.	Did not describe topic. Little or poor organization/ preparation. Some factual errors.	Demonstrated some knowledge of subject. Lacked basic information or some part of presentation i.e. beginning or ending.	Showed preparation and knowledge of subject. Major points were discussed. Talk was organized and easy to follow.	Informative, organized, well rehearsed and interesting. All major aspects presented and thoroughly discussed. Speaker used visuals to reinforce and clarify.		
Written aspect	No report submitted.	Incomplete. Some factual errors. Sloppy work with spelling errors. Copied from references.	Incomplete. Some basic understanding of the topic. Inadequate use of references.	Report was completely done and covered the main points. Work was neat, spelling was correct. Sentences were used. Resources included.	Report was neat, complete, descriptive, well organized and well written. Went beyond the basic assignment to explain topics. Several references cited.		
Work habits	Unfocused. No effort to utilize time productively to do assigned work.	Poor use of time for research and study. Not on task much of the time.	Had difficulty getting started. Needed continued assistance in using resources. Use of time and focus on task is improving.	Made good use of time to research and study with little guidance. Able to work quietly and on task without reminders. Asked for assistance when needed.	Showed independent, focused use of study time. Took advantage of multiple resources without assistance. Effective use of time.		
Total							

Rubric Score	Comment	Grade
19 - 20	Excellent	A+
17 - 18	Very Good	A
15 - 16	Good	B+
13 - 14	Good	B
10 - 12	Fair	C+
6 - 9	Fair	C
3 - 5	Unsatisfactory	D (U)
0 - 2	Unsatisfactory	F (U)

ANALYTIC RUBRIC FOR A MULTI-MODAL PROJECT

Criteria	0	Beginning 1	Progressing 2	Proficient 3	Superior 4	Student assessment	Teacher assessment
Visual aspect							
Oral aspect							
Written aspect							
Work habits							
Total							

Rubric Score	Comment	Grade
	Excellent	A+
	Very Good	A
	Good	B+
	Good	B
	Fair	C+
	Fair	C
	Unsatisfactory	D (U)
	Unsatisfactory	F (U)

BEHAVIORAL RUBRIC

Criteria	1	2	3	4	Student assessment	Teacher assessment
Performance on assigned work	Does not perform task or performs without evidence of skill.	Performs task with minimal evidence of skill.	Performs task with moderate level of skill.	Performs task with superior level of skill.		
Appropriateness of behavior during assigned work	Is not age-appropriate. Persistent challenging behaviors.	Sometimes appropriate. Minimal conformance to expectations.	Usually appropriate. Generally meets established behavioral expectations.	Continually very appropriate.		
Level of assistance needed to do assigned work	Unable or unwilling to perform independently. Needs maximum supervision.	Performs with direct assistance and some support.	Follows instructions and responds independently.	Independent. Completes assigned tasks in exemplary manner without supervision and in timely fashion.		
Total Points						

BEHAVIORAL RUBRIC

Criteria	1	2	3	4	Student assessment	Teacher assessment
Performance on assigned work						
Appropriateness of behavior during assigned work						
Level of assistance needed to do assigned work						
Total Points						

STUDENT PORTFOLIO RUBRIC

	Beginning 1	Progressing 2	Proficient 3	Superior 4	Score
Academing Standards	Does not meet objectives or expectations.	Minimally meets expectations.	Meets most academic expectations.	Meets all or nearly all academic expectations.	
Performance	Student demonstrates no evidence of meeting targeted IEP goal(s). Content, process and product are not age appropriate.	Student is moving toward meeting IEP goal(s). Content, process or products are becoming age-appropriate.	Student demonstrates increased progress toward meeting targeted IEP goals in an age appropriate manner.	Student demonstrates ability to meet targeted IEP goals; content, process and product are age appropriate.	
Settings	Student is unable to perform targeted IEP goals or participates or performs in a limited number of settings and situations.	Student performs targeted IEP goals in a number of settings and situations.	Student performs targeted IEP goals in a wide variety of settings and situations.	Student demonstrates mastery in performance of targeted IEP goals in diverse settings and situations.	
Support	No evidence of the use of peer support or appropriate assistive technology. Does not demonstrate ability/interest in planning, monitoring or evaluating.	Makes limited use of peer supports and demonstrates limited use of assistive technology, planning, monitoring or evaluating.	Makes appropriate use of peer support, assistive technology; demonstrates use of planning, monitoring and evaluating.	Demonstrates appropriate use of all supports; shows independence in work: demonstrates effectiveness in planning, monitoring and evaluating.	
Social Relationships	Student has limited social interactions.	Student has appropriate social interactions with a small range of peers.	Student has sustained, appropriate and reciprocal social interactions with a range of peers.	Student has sustained social relationships to include choice interaction with 'friends'; has a developed social network.	
Self - Determination	Student makes limited or no choice in development of portfolio product; planning, monitoring and evaluation are poor or non existent.	Student makes minimal learning choices in portfolio products; planning, monitoring or evaluating own performance is inconsistent.	Student consistently makes learning choices; consistently plans, monitors and evaluates performance.	Student makes wise choices related to personal learning; consistently plans, monitors and evaluates own performance; uses evaluation to improve and/or set goals.	
Total					

STUDENT PORTFOLIO RUBRIC

	Beginning 1	Progressing 2	Proficient 3	Superior 4	Score
Academing Standards					
Performance					
Settings					
Support					
Social Relationships					
Self - Determination					
Total					

Dear Teachers,

Set the climate and standard for professional assessment. Establish measurable goals and objectives. Take time to regularly assess. Discuss the strengths and weaknesses that are revealed. Determine to build on the strengths.

The following section offers you TIPS to assist in personal and collaborative assessment essential for growth. Utilize the forms to encourage open, critical reflection, comments and suggestions, from both co-teachers and from students! Don't be afraid to take a little of the assessment 'medicine' you so readily hand out. Indeed, here is an opportunity to become assessment role models for your students.

Sincerely,

June

Teacher and Coteacher Assessment

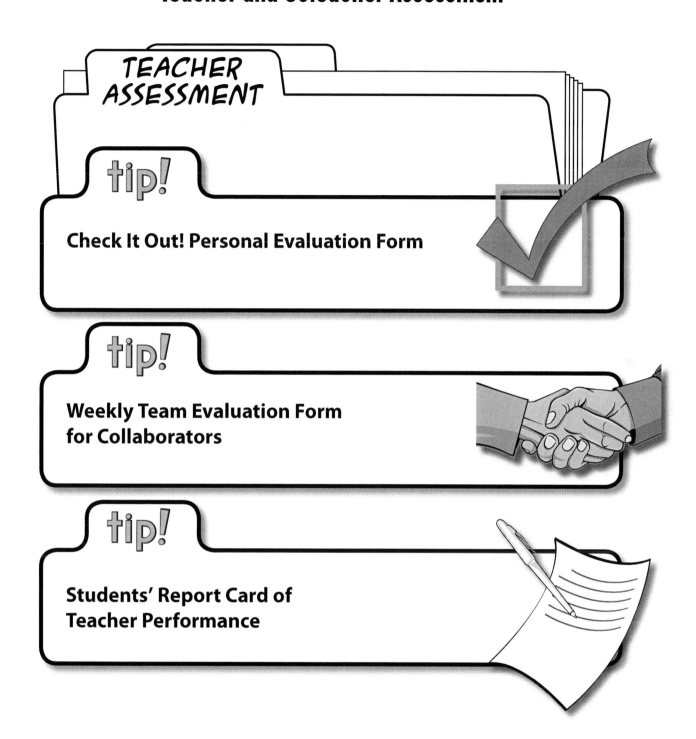

TEACHER ASSESSMENT

tip!

Check It Out! Personal Evaluation Form

tip!

Weekly Team Evaluation Form
for Collaborators

tip!

Students' Report Card of
Teacher Performance

PERSONAL EVALUATION FORM
Are You Encouraging Collaborating Growth?

	Great	Fair	Poor
Treat your co-teacher(s) with courtesy and respect both in and out of the classroom.			
Do more than your share, voluntarily.			
Determine and utilize a regular and mutually convenient time for lesson planning.			
Keep the planning time focused and be professional on needs of all students.			
Welcome of the collaborator(s) with a smile, tone of voice, body language and actions daily.			
Share space, emotional and physical, for the comfort and convenience of my collaborator(s).			
Show genuine interest in the collaborator(s), personally and professionally.			
Actively listen to verbal and non-verbal messages and respond appropriately.			
Resist temptation to judge or criticize.			
Regularly evaluate personal and collaborative success objectively; state concerns positively.			
Fulfill mutually agreed upon professional responsibilities including full responsibility in the event of coteacher's absence.			
Demonstrate flexibility in changing direction.			
Laugh, especially at self.			
Demonstrate regular and punctual attendance. If possible, arrive early to set up and prepare for students.			
Plan and prepare lessons collaboratively.			
Secure and set up the necessary audio-visual equipment.			
Follow through on the agreed upon behavioral expectations (yours, your co-teacher(s) and students).			
Follow through on the agreed upon academic expectations, initial evaluation criteria (yours, your coteacher(s) and students).			

My greatest strengths are:

_____

_____

_____

Areas in which I can improve include:

_____

_____

_____

WEEKLY TEAM EVALUATION FOR COLLABORATORS

Evaluate collaborative progress informally and continually. Use this guide to help improve your efforts to objectively discuss your collaborative work.

Check It Off!

1 = Strongly agree
2 = Agree
3 = Unsure
4 = Disagree
5 = Strongly disagree

	1	2	3	4	5
The inclusion lessons were well planned and implemented.					
Instruction in the class was collaboratively agreed upon as well as the coteaching roles.					
The coteaching styles worked well together. (Why/why not/ when?).					
Special education students benefited from the instruction. (If not, why not? What could have been done differently?)					
Regular education students benefited from the instruction. (If not, why not? What could have been done differently?)					
The special education teacher planned and implemented necessary modifications to instruction to meet student needs.					
The special education teacher provided necessary modified materials to meet student needs.					
Curricular modifications and planning were appropriate for all students.					
IEP mandates were considered and implemented.					
Communication with all students was fair, appropriate and effective.					
There was consistency in dealing with rules and enforcing discipline. The coteaching team worked together on classroom management.					
The general and special educators communicated differences and concerns in a constructive and respectful manner.					
Team members were flexible in adjusting assignments, in curricular planning and determining instructional strategies.					
The collaborating team projects a coordinated and positive feeling about inclusion.					
Assessment was ongoing and appropriate and used to modify instruction and for remediation.					

1. At this time, what are the strong points of our collaborative effort?

_____

_____

2. At this time, what are the weak points of our collaborative effort?

_____

_____

3. At this time, how can our team better prepare, accomplish curricular objectives and work more effectively?

_____

_____

_____

STUDENTS' REPORT CARD OF TEACHER PERFORMANCE
CHECK YOUR TEACHER OUT!

Consider having your students *anonymously grade your report card* at the end of each marking period. Students can offer insights into teaching strengths and weaknesses, which can foster professional growth. Allow them to create their evaluation system if the one below does not suit their needs.

	Needs Improvement F	Poor D	Fair C	Good B	Excellent A
Knowledge of subject					
Interesting and clear presentation of subject					
Appropriateness of work to needs of students					
Appropriateness of work to curriculum					
Behavior toward students					
Behavior toward coteachers					
Management/disciplinary matters					
Sets high standards					
Motivates/offers encouragement and support					
Availability for extra help					
Appropriate assessment of student work and behavior					
Contact with home					

Comments:

_____

_____

_____

_____

_____

_____

_____

STUDENTS' REPORT CARD OF TEACHER PERFORMANCE

	Needs Improvement F	Poor D	Fair C	Good B	Excellent A
Knowledge of subject					
Interesting and clear presentation of subject					
Appropriateness of work to needs of students					
Appropriateness of work to curriculum					
Behavior toward students					
Behavior toward coteachers					
Management/disciplinary matters					
Sets high standards					
Motivates/offers encouragement and support					
Availability for extra help					
Appropriate assessment of student work and behavior					
Contact with home					

Comments:

_____

_____

_____

_____

_____

_____

_____

_____

ALTERNATE ASSESSMENT 5

Dear Teachers,

Perhaps your administrator is calling upon you to develop and implement some form of alternate assessment for your most cognitively disabled students. Your response is, "But what does that mean and how do I do it?"

If you are stressed trying to figure out how to proceed with alternate assessment, let this next section help you. There are TIPS to explain what, how and why. Importantly, there are alternative options that are currently used and samples to show you how to get started. Moreover, there are some cautionary suggestions to keep you focused as you take on the task of alternate assessment.

Sincerely,

June

Alternate Assessment

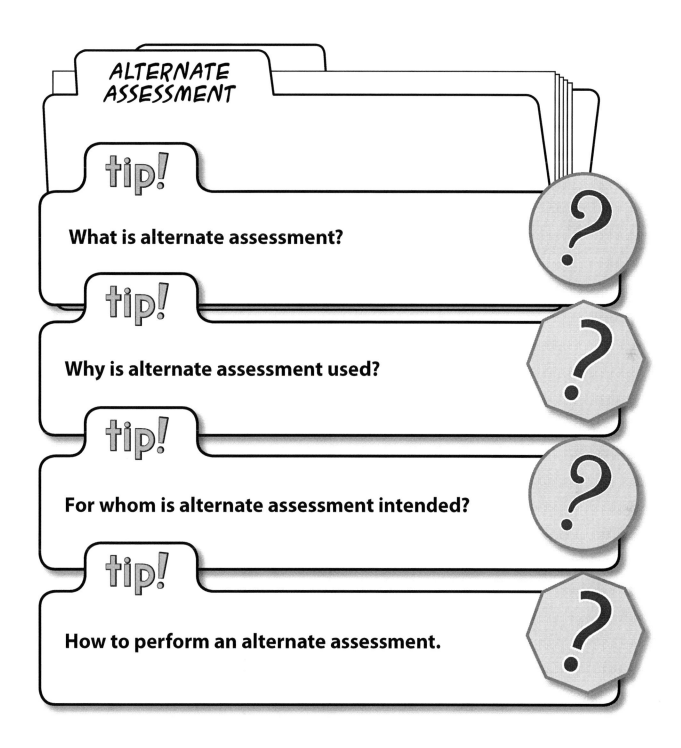

ALTERNATE ASSESSMENT

tip!

What is alternate assessment?

tip!

Why is alternate assessment used?

tip!

For whom is alternate assessment intended?

tip!

How to perform an alternate assessment.

ALTERNATE ASSESSMENT

What is it?

- Assessment geared for targeted special needs students.

- Assessment developed for use in those situations when standard formal assessment is deemed inappropriate, even with accommodations.

- Assessment tool(s) to provide information regarding the progress of targeted special needs students.

- Assessment developed in an effort to determine program/subject matter suitability for targeted special needs students.

- Assessment developed in an effort to provide an appropriate means to evaluate the progress of targeted special needs students.

- Assessment relating to the general curriculum and to IEP goals.

Why Is Alternative Assessment Used?

- Federal law mandates it.

- To give a picture of how students with severe disabilities are performing.

- Most formal assessments are unfair and inappropriate for the severely cognitively impaired special needs students.

- Law allows for more realistic tools to determine progress of targeted special needs students.

- Primarily to give a more realistic picture of how a school, district, or state is doing in terms of overall student performance in order to hold them accountable.

- To allow special needs students with diverse abilities to demonstrate problem solving skills and the opportunity to meet established goals in order to participate more fully in the general education curriculum.

Adapted Brynes, (2004)

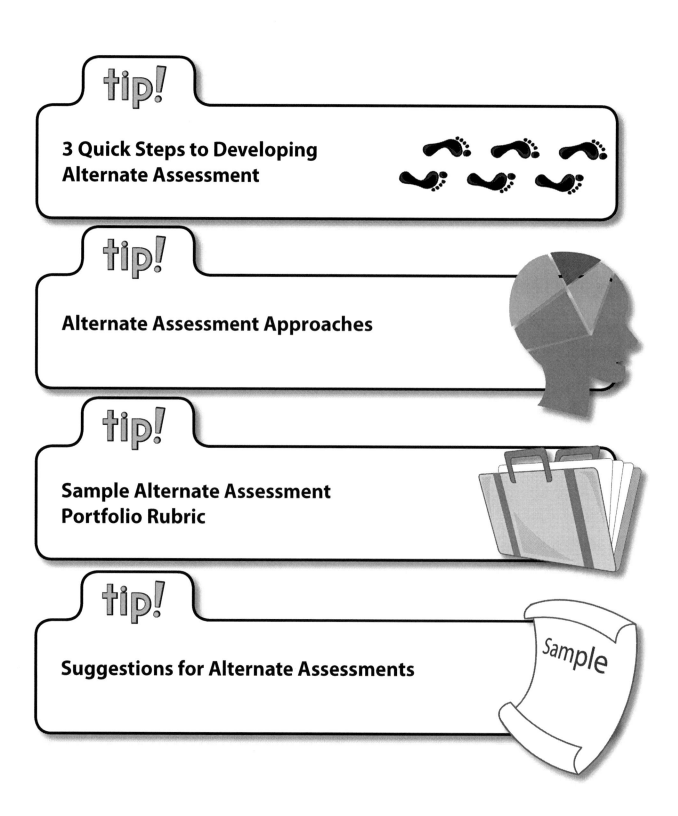

tip!

3 Quick Steps to Developing Alternate Assessment

tip!

Alternate Assessment Approaches

tip!

Sample Alternate Assessment Portfolio Rubric

tip!

Suggestions for Alternate Assessments

Sample

3 STEPS

1. Identify qualified students as stated in the IEPs.

2. Clarify district alternative assessment approach (see options on following page). Focus on identified approach.

3. Develop a rubric for scoring. Collect ongoing data to support objectives. Store in an appropriate place.

DEVELOPING AN ALTERNATIVE ASSESSMENT
Alternate Assessment Approaches

Portfolio – An on-going collection of student work such as samples of written assignments, tests, drawings, videos, observations and checklists that span a period of time and demonstrate student performance and learning. Portfolio samples focus on specific skills or content areas that usually relate to state standards. A predetermined scoring method is used for assessment purposes (usually in rubric form).

IEP Linked Collection of Evidence – Similar to a portfolio. It is a sample collection of student work that demonstrates student achievement on standards-based IEP goals and objectives. A predetermined assessment method is used to measure performance as compared to specific scoring criteria (usually in rubric form).

Performance Assessment – The student is given a specific task to perform, usually in a one to one situation with a teacher. The teacher observes student performance and measures degree of mastery. A predetermined assessment method is used to measure level of performance as compared to specific scoring criteria (usually in rubric form).

Checklist – Student skill performance level is assessed on a pre-determined body of skills by a person who works with or has observed the student in a variety of situations, videotaped or audio-taped the student or interviewed the student/family members. The checklist generally includes items related to degree of independence/support, appropriateness of relationships, generalization across settings as well as performance on assigned work. Scoring generally involves determining the number and degree to which student was able to perform checklist items and in what settings and for what purpose.

Traditional (pencil/paper or computer) Test – The more 'typical test' can be administered in a one on one situation, small group setting or large group with support as required. The teacher may read the questions, and help with the recording of responses (providing student IEP testing modifications). Assessment may allow for the elimination of certain test items deemed inappropriate for the student (dependent upon student IEP testing modifications).

STUDENT PORTFOLIO RUBRIC

	Beginning 1	Progressing 2	Proficient 3	Superior 4	Score
ACADEMIC STANDARDS	Does not meet objectives or expectations.	Minimally meets expectations	Meets most academic expectations.	Meets all or nearly all academic expectations.	
PERFORMANCE	Student demonstrates no evidence of meeting targeted IEP goal(s). Content, process and product are not age appropriate.	Student is moving toward meeting IEP goal(s). Content, process or products are becoming age-appropriate.	Student demonstrates increased progress toward meeting targeted IEP goals in an age appropriate manner.	Student demonstrates ability to meet targeted IEP goals; content, process and product are age appropriate.	
SETTINGS	Student is unable to perform targeted IEP goals or participates or performs in a limited number of settings and situations.	Student performs targeted IEP goals in a small number of settings and situations.	Student performs targeted IEP goals in a wide variety of settings and situations.	Student demonstrates mastery in performance of targeted IEP goals in diverse settings and situations.	
SUPPORT	No evidence of the use of peer support or appropriate assistive technology. Does not demonstrate ability/interest in planning, monitoring or evaluating.	Makes limited use of peer supports and demonstrates limited use of assistive technology; limited planning, monitoring or evaluating.	Makes appropriate use of peer support, assistive technology; demonstrates use of planning, monitoring and evaluating.	Demonstrates appropriate use of all supports. Shows independence in work: demonstrates effectiveness in planning, monitoring and evaluating.	
SOCIAL RELATIONSHIPS	Student has limited social interactions.	Student has appropriate social interactions with a small range of peers.	Student has sustained, appropriate and reciprocal social interactions with a range of peers.	Student has sustained social relationships to include choice interaction with 'friends'; has a developed social network.	
SELF-DETERMINATION	Student makes limited or no choice in development of portfolio product; planning, monitoring and evaluation are poor or none existent.	Student makes minimal learning choices in portfolio products; planning, monitoring or evaluating own performance is inconsistent.	Student consistently makes learning choices; consistently plans, monitors and evaluates performance.	Student makes wise choices related to personal learning; consistently plans, monitors and evaluates own performance; uses evaluation to improve and/or set goals.	
TOTAL					

Adapted from: http://rubistar.4teachers.org

STUDENT PORTFOLIO RUBRIC

	BEGINNING 1	PROGRESSING 2	PROFICIENT 3	SUPERIOR 4	SCORE
ACADEMIC STANDARDS					
PERFORMANCE					
SETTINGS					
SUPPORT					
SOCIAL RELATIONSHIPS					
SELF-DETERMINATION					
TOTAL					

Adapted from: http://rubistar.4teachers.org

RECOMMENDATIONS FOR ALTERNATE ASSESSMENTS

Consider These Suggestions...

The following four recommendations have helped to shape state criteria decisions on alternate assessment in recognition of the need for appropriate instruction and meaningful assessment of the most impaired of special needs students.

1. Focus on skills related to community living and real life situations and settings.

2. Measure the extent to which performance can be generalized across a variety of settings. Try to make assessment on going rather than a one-time affair.

3. Review and assess the extent to which the system (district, school, teacher) provides student supports and modifications as well as prepares the student to use them.

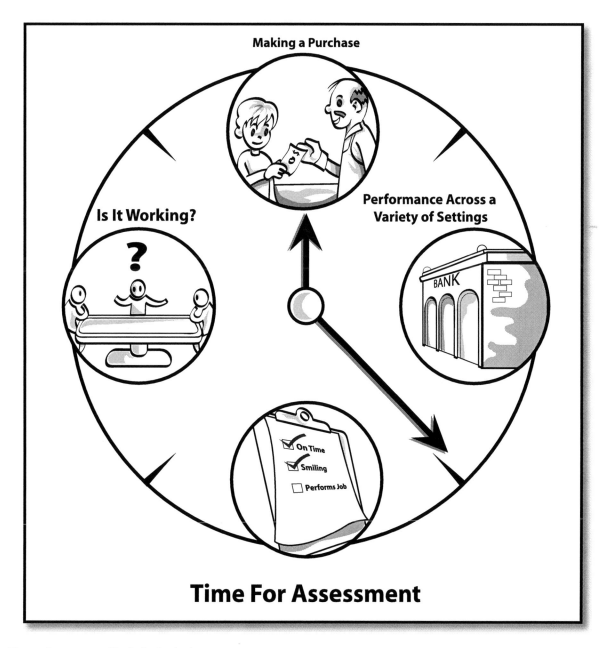

Time For Assessment

WHO IS ALTERNATE ASSESSMENT FOR?

For Whom?

- **No Child Left Behind** legislation limits the use of alternate assessment to only those students most significantly cognitively impaired.

- The IEP team determines eligibility of special needs students.

- Classroom teachers implement alternate assessment but do not determine student eligibility.

- Generally less than 1% of the total population assessed in a large-scale assessment.

Adapted from: http://education.umn.edu/NCEO/

How To Do Alternative Assessment?

- No single model or set of standards exists.

- Educators express confusion and concern about appropriate construction, especially without adequate training and support.

- Use criteria that represent the desired successful special needs student outcomes, i.e. a set of skills, level of independence, ability to get along, ability to develop and maintain relationships etc.

- Relate criteria to specific goals and standards set forth in IEPs and generally linked to state content standards.

Adapted from: http://education.umn.edu/NCEO/

Dear Teachers,

The students in your inclusion class will have a wide range of abilities and disabilities, academic and behavioral. You must teach all of them to the state standards while preparing them for rigorous end-of-year exams. How can your year-round testing provide you with the necessary information about their subject mastery?

This testing section of Briefcase Three has been designed to give you TIPS on all aspects of testing for the inclusion class. It is meant to prepare you to test all of your students more fairly in a less stressful manner.

Sincerely,

June

Testing in the Inclusion Classroom

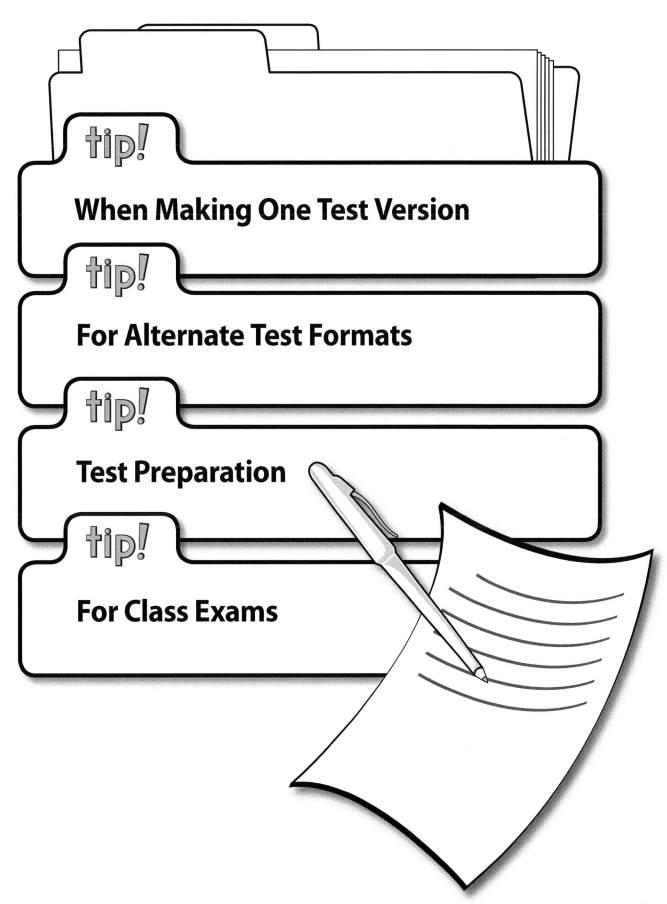

tip!

When Making One Test Version

tip!

For Alternate Test Formats

tip!

Test Preparation

tip!

For Class Exams

TIPS FOR TESTING THE MULTI-LEVEL CLASS

CAUTION!
Always provide IEP mandated testing modifications for all special needs students.

The Dozen Recipe: One Test Version

Start Easy!

Start with easier questions at the beginning of the test and increase the level of difficulty toward the end of the test.

Simple Directions!

Make the directions simple. Consider enlarging or bolding important words. Repeat directions if section carries over to another page.

Avoid Never!

Avoid using "always, never, not, except." Avoid "all of the above," "some of the above" and "none of the above."

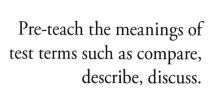

Compare, Describe, Discuss!

Pre-teach the meanings of test terms such as compare, describe, discuss.

Place all matching items
on one page.
Minimize choices.

Avoid having students transfer
answers to another page.

Double-space tests with
an uncluttered look.

Arrange multiple-choice options vertically.
Use numbers rather than letters that might
confuse the dyslexic student. Whenever
possible limit it to only 3 choices.

Avoid long, wordy questions.
Test concepts rather than reading
vocabulary.

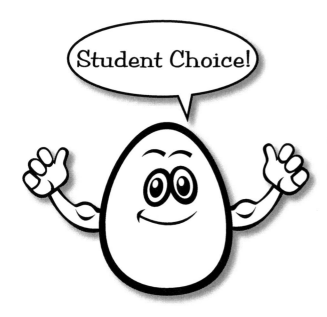

Provide opportunities for students to skip one question in each section.

Provide 'bonus' or 'challenge' opportunities in each section.

Consider allowing students to write a paragraph detailing and supporting their understanding of a given topic related to the unit of study.

TIPS FOR TESTING THE MULTI-LEVEL CLASS

Ensure that all students have a quiet, distraction-free testing space.

The Half Dozen Recipe: Alternate Test Formats

Make tiered versions of the exam. Increase the level of difficulty in vocabulary, concept and response expectation as you progress from a lower level to a higher-level tier.

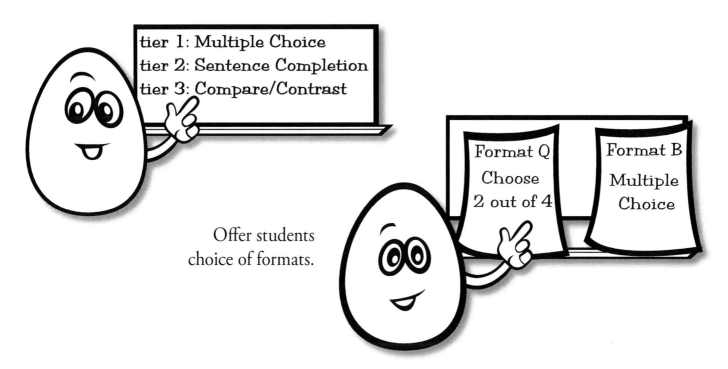

tier 1: Multiple Choice
tier 2: Sentence Completion
tier 3: Compare/Contrast

Offer students choice of formats.

Format Q
Choose 2 out of 4

Format B
Multiple Choice

Clearly identify that the degree of difficulty and the degree of accuracy determines the point range.

Regular   High Test   Premium

MC 1pts   Fill ins 1.5 pts   Essays 5 pts

WHAT'S IN YOUR TANK?

USE CONTRACTS OR INDEPENDENT ASSIGNMENTS

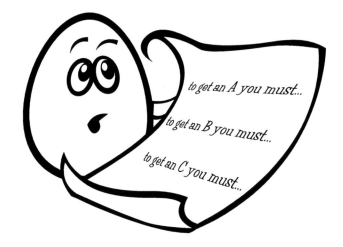

to get an A you must...

to get an B you must...

to get an C you must...

Make versions of tests specifically for different students. Distribute the more challenging test version to the more advanced students.

Test 1

Test 2

MAKE VERSIONS OF TESTS

Consider allowing targeted special needs students to tape record responses.

CONSIDER TAPE RECORDING RESPONSES

PREPARING STUDENTS FOR TESTS

Let there be no surprises, no gotchas! Students who know what to expect and who have seen and practiced on exams of similar difficulty levels tend to have less test anxiety and tend to score better.

REVIEW AND PRACTICE

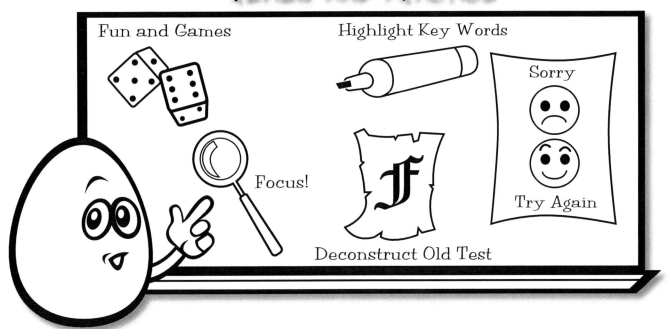

1. Practice questions similar to test items prior to the test. Use them in a game format similar to Jeopardy.

2. Develop "focus activities" using test type questions. Have students practice critiquing and allocating points for answers.

3. Deconstruct previous state and local exams. Use questions as homework items. Score the responses in class showing how to attain maximum credit.

4. Encourage students to use highlighters on key words or phrases in directions or in questions.

5. Use tests as teaching tools. Allow a 'retake' of the test in an alternate format after re-teaching concepts/questions of concern.

MORE TEST TIPS FOR THE MULTI-LEVEL CLASS

1. Encourage students to answer 'easy' questions first, to unlock test anxiety.

2. Practice essay questions. Have students get in the habit of writing down 'X' number of important points in phrase form then convert to paragraph form.

3. Train students to monitor their time, spending the most time on questions worth the most points. Include point allocations on tests. Call student attention to the areas of highest value.

4. Develop a specialized subject area vocabulary. Use spare moments for review or have a 'gaming period' for vocabulary and concept review prior to the test.

5. Develop and encourage student use of well-organized study guides that complement lectures, class work and readings. Have students 'make up' test questions for class to practice answering

TEACHING TEST TAKING STRATEGIES

TIPS FOR IN-CLASS TEACHER-MADE TESTS

TIPS FOR CLASS EXAMS

1. Develop the expectation of timely correction and return of papers and that exams will be used as a teaching tool.

2. Consider grading test paper after the student makes corrections and hands it in the second time. Grade all corrected portions with ½ credits rather than no credit.

3. Grade as soon as possible after collecting tests, preferably with the student present.

4. You grade or the student grades, not a classmate.

5. If test results are very poor, reteach and then retest.

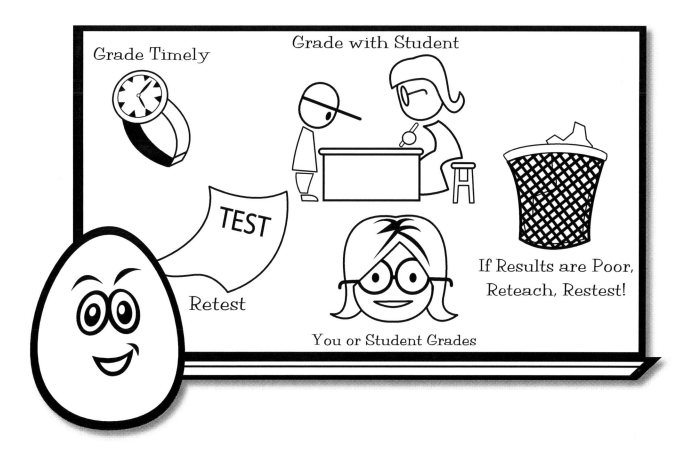

MORE TIPS FOR IN-CLASS TEACHER-MADE TESTS

1. Analyze class test results. Remediate aspects that were frequently missed.

2. Occasionally give an open book test.

3. Consider giving a performance assessment to replace a written test. Be consistent in scoring. Preferably use a rubric to objectify scoring.

4. Keep standards and expectations high and in line with your report card grading criteria.

5. Encourage students to compare and contrast their current test performance with previous work.

Dear Teachers,

It's one thing to give a test, it's another thing to assign a grade. Grading for the inclusion teacher, especially report card grading, is difficult. Grading not only communicates information about the student, it also communicates information about the teacher(s).

Collaborative decisions about grading require agreement on basic philosophy and professional objectives. Let this section of grading TIPS help you and your coteacher(s) with this thorny issue.

Sincerely,

June

Grading in the Inclusion Class

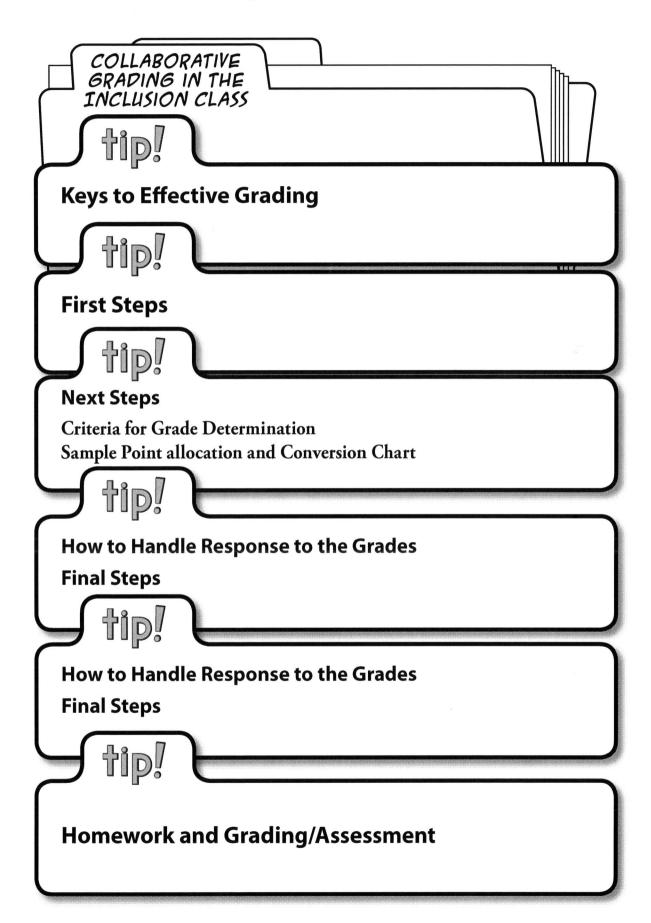

COLLABORATIVE GRADING IN THE INCLUSION CLASS

tip!

Keys to Effective Grading

tip!

First Steps

tip!

Next Steps

Criteria for Grade Determination
Sample Point allocation and Conversion Chart

tip!

How to Handle Response to the Grades

Final Steps

tip!

How to Handle Response to the Grades

Final Steps

tip!

Homework and Grading/Assessment

COLLABORATIVE GRADING IN THE INCLUSION CLASS

Collaborative agreement on a grading policy is not an easy process. Try to stay focused on the goal: Objectively and accurately reporting the performance of your diverse student learners.

- **Make an effort to communicate growth, progress and level of mastery.**

- **Be objective.**

- **Be truthful and fair.**

- **Be consistent with school policy and IEP guidelines.**

- **Clearly and accurately communicate student performance.**

- **Be readily understood by student and parents.**

- **Use multiple assessment tools.**

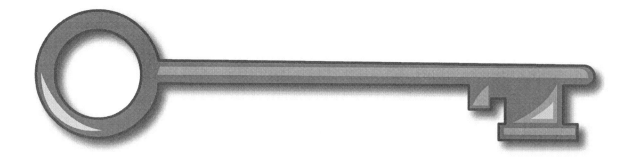

First Steps in Inclusion Grading

- Know the existing school/district grading policy.
  (Must be in alignment with those as well as federal and state mandates.)

- Check the IEP guidelines for special needs students to honor those mandates.

- Keep the focus on the students.

- Individually consider your grading philosophy.
  What are the 'musts' in it?

- Discuss the 'musts' of your coteacher(s) grading philosophy.

- Determine common threads. Identify areas of concerns.

- Work toward a mutually acceptable agreement.

- Be patient. If necessary, take several sessions of brainstorming before deciding.

- If decision is difficult, seek help from a colleague/administrator to listen and assist you in arriving in a satisfactory policy.

- Establish a rubric with a list of your criteria to objectify the grading procedure.

- Assign a point value to each of the criteria. Use point spread to assign grades.

Next Steps

Criteria/Points for Grade Determination

Criteria	Points
Test/retest grades	7
Quiz grades	1
Notebook check	1
Group work	1
Independent work	1
Research projects	1
Presentations	2
Class discussions and participation	2
Daily homework completion	1
Class work assignments	2
Extra credit project	2
Performance assessment	2
Demonstrations	2
Total	**25**

Conversion Chart

Points	Comment	Grade
24 - 25	Excellent	A - A+
21 - 23	Good	B - B+
17 - 20	Fair	C - C+
15 - 16	Needs Improvement	D
0 - 14	Unsatisfactory	F

Next Steps

Criteria/Points for Grade Determination

Criteria	Points
Total	

Conversion Chart

Points	Comment	Grade
	Excellent	A - A+
	Good	B - B+
	Fair	C - C+
	Needs Improvement	D
	Unsatisfactory	F

HOW TO HANDLE STUDENT RESPONSE TO GRADES

- Set aside time to discuss the grading policy with parents and students.

- Listen carefully and answer concerns.

- Be certain to be positive with students who have worked but are disappointed with their grade.

- Remind students of specifics of how they have overcome academic challenges previously.

- Offer definite suggestions showing how students might overcome challenges and improve their grade.

- Plan to monitor 'students of concern' and provide support through the marking period.

HELPFUL HINTS FOR INCLUSION GRADING

Suggested Do's and Don'ts for Inclusion Grading

Try to	Avoid
Offer mandated testing modifications in the least intrusive and obtrusive manner possible.	Calling attention to those students in need of testing modifications.
Give positive feedback when possible, for example: Great job on the writing part of the test. You gave 4 important facts.	Posting grades or reading grades aloud.
Encourage oral presentations (formal or informal).	Penalizing the unsure or quiet student who prefers not to or refuses to participate.
Use multiple assessment techniques.	Using only one measure for determining grades.
Encourage creative ways to demonstrate mastery.	Expecting all students to perform well on pencil/paper tests.
Give several shorter or less extensive tests more frequently.	Give one long, intensive and extensive test.
Grade papers yourself or have students grade their own papers.	Having students grade another's work.
Grade notebooks of folders for completion and neatness.	No expectation of keeping notes and notebooks up to date.
Include bonus questions for all and/or challenge questions for those more able.	Tests constructed at a single level of challenge.

MORE SUGGESTIONS: DO'S AND DON'TS FOR INCLUSION GRADING

Try to	Avoid
Consider a 'fun' question to reduce test-taking stress.	Hand-written or poorly formatted exams.
Review before the test day. Construct tests from study outlines of concepts and terms.	Using tests made by peers that do not reflect your teaching.
Answer subject matter questions prior to disbursing tests.	Introducing any new material on test day.
Use tests as teaching tools for unit exams or high stakes exams.	Using grades as threats.
Allow for retake of test in an alternate format. Allow students to correct test items and resubmit, consider giving partial credit for corrected items.	Using tests as an end rather than a means to improve learning.
Give an open notebook or take home test.	Giving unclear directions on tests or imprecise information about grading policy.
Allow students to practice devising test items and answering them.	Having students grade another's work.
Allow time to practice using new test formats prior to the testing day.	Making the test cumbersome and difficult to determine how or where to answer questions. The need for students to transfer information from one paper to another.
Keep a quiet, non-threatening testing environment.	Talking or allowing others to talk during testing.
Accept and encourage critical suggestions about grading techniques and policy from students and parents.	Being rigid, positional and defensive about the grading techniques and policy.
Provide opportunities for small group work (i.e.. all brainstorm 'a problem', one records, one reports to the class.)	Relying on one piece of individual work as the sole determinant for a grade.

Stride (2005)

WHAT PART DOES HOMEWORK PLAY IN GRADING AND ASSESSMENT?

What about Homework and Assessment?

- Homework can help to improve student performance when appropriately designed to match student abilities and to relate to class instruction.

- Homework can help both student and teacher informally assess student learning while increasing achievement.

- Homework is most effective when the reading level is slightly below the student's ability level.

- Teachers have found that well developed homework can promote understanding of what students are learning and what they still need to learn.

- Homework can effectively amplify student learning and help prepare students for class discussions, if the assignments are correlated with daily lessons.

- There seems to be a direct relationship between homework completion and homework effectiveness when teachers regularly collect, discuss and provide feedback on homework.

- Homework reveals academic effort and work in progress, not a final product.

- Homework effort and completion can be used effectively to complement class work and be a component of grading.

- Homework should not be the primary measure for determining a final grade.

Dear Teachers,

Why on earth would a teacher even consider evaluating their program? Doesn't he/she have enough to do? Further, it is not mandated. Indeed, generally, it is not even expected. So, why do it?

I'm certain you know the answer. The professional educator wants to make a positive difference, academically and behaviorally, in the lives of their students. Program evaluation enables teachers to determine whether their time and effort is effecting a positive change. If so, what aspects are effective and what aspects need altering?

This section of Briefcase Three will provide you with TIPS and alternative approaches for your program evaluation. Our recommendation is to begin simple and small and grow as you gain confidence.

Sincerely,

June

Program Evaluation

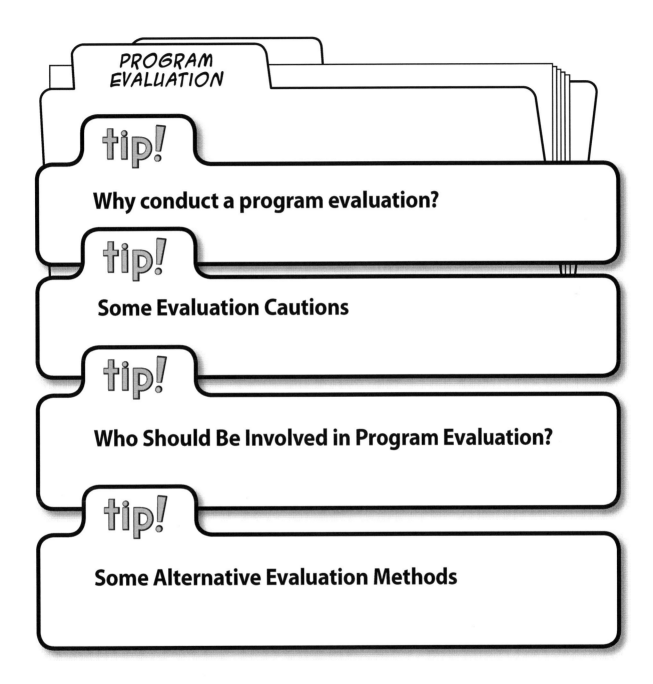

PROGRAM
EVALUATION

tip!

Why conduct a program evaluation?

tip!

Some Evaluation Cautions

tip!

Who Should Be Involved in Program Evaluation?

tip!

Some Alternative Evaluation Methods

Why Evaluate?

- To determine the effectiveness of your program.

- To determine the effectiveness of your instruction.

- To determine the relationship between student performance and your program.

- To determine the extent to which your program is aligned with state standards.

- To determine the impact instruction has had on student skills, performance and behavior.

- To determine the reactions and feelings of others (administration, students, parents, colleagues) about your program.

- To determine how to move forward in a more effective manner.

MORE PROGRAM EVALUATION

Cautionary TIPS

- There is NO one right or wrong way for program evaluation.

- Start with your goals: Why are you evaluating?

- Build your evaluation around your goals.

- Start with the KISS *(Keep It Simple Stupid)* principal in mind.

- Start small.

- Don't expect perfection.

- Include some questionnaires/interviews so that you can get the more in-depth responses.

- Be ready to accept critical comments and negative responses. Honest criticism helps you find HOW and in WHAT ways to grow.

- Be on the look out for data that shows strengths, weaknesses and ways to improve.

- Encourage anonymity for honesty of response.

Who Should Be Involved?

After you determine your purpose and goals select the audience that can best help give you the desired information.

Consider involving:

- Colleagues
- Administrators
- Counselors
- Paraprofessionals
- Parents
- Students
- Ancillary staff

OUR PRINCIPAL
MRS. CLARKE

OUR SECRETARIES
MISS ARNOLD   MRS. MARQUEZ

OUR NURSE
MRS. TOBIAS

OUR CAFETERIA WORKER
MRS. QUINN

OUR SECURITY GUARD
MR GIVENS

OUR GUIDANCE COUNSELOR
MRS DONNELY

OUR PSYCHOLOGIST
MR JEFFERIES

OUR LIBRARY STAFF
MR SWITZER

OUR COMPUTER LAB STAFF
MR FRANK   MISS MONTEGOMERY

OUR CUSTODIAN
MR LEONARDI

STUDENTS

JAMAL HARRIS

KAREN COOPER

RUTH PRICE

JENNIFER EISNER

SARAH FONG

CARSON BUCK

DAVID MEYERS

PEDRO RUIZ

Alternative Methods for Program Evaluation

- Questionnaires
- Focus groups
- Narratives
- Interviews
- Surveys
- Documentation review (from records)
- Case studies
- Observations
- Checklists

RESOURCES

Bradley, D. (Nov/Dec 1998). Grading modified assignments: Equity or compromise, Teaching Exceptional Children 31(2), 24-29.

Brualdi, A. (1998). Implementing performance assessment in the classroom. Practical Assessment, Research & Evaluation 6(2).

Byrnes, M. (July/August, 2004). Alternate assessment FAQs (and answers), Teaching Exceptional Children v36(6), 59-63.

Calkins, L., Montgomery, K., and Santman, D. (1999). Helping children master the tricks and avoid the traps of standardized tests, A Teacher's Guide to Standardized Reading Tests. Knowledge is Power. Portsmouth, NH: Heinemann.

Christensen, J. (Nov/Dec 1998). A decision for grading students. Teaching Exceptional Children. 31(2), 30-35.

Heubcrt, J.P. (2002). High-stakes testing: Opportunities and risks for students of color, English-language learners and students with disabilities, The Continuing Challenge; Moving the Youth Agenda Forward. Baltimore, MD: Johns Hopkins University Press.

Klingner, J. and Vaughn, S. (Fall 1999). Students' perceptions of instruction in inclusion classrooms: Implications for students with learning disabilities, Exceptional Children, v66(n1), 23-37.

Linn, R. L. (2000). Assessments and accountability, Educational Researcher 29(2), 4-16.

Mertler, C. A. (2001). Designing scoring rubrics for your classroom. Practical Assessment, Research & Evaluation, 7(25).

Olson, L. (2004). 'Value added' models gain in popularity. Retrieved from *http://www.edweek.org/ew/news/teaching-and-learning/*.

Starin, S. Functional Behavioral Assessments: What, Why, When, Where, and Who? Retrieved from *http://www.wrightslaw.com*.

Stride, J. (2004). Practical Strategies for including high school students with behavioral disabilities. Verona, WI: IEP Resources.

Stride, J. (2005). Practical Strategies for elementary inclusion. Verona, WI: IEP Resources.

Tienken, C. and Wilson, M. (2001). Using state standards and tests to improve instruction, Practical Assessment. Research & Evaluation, 7(13).

US Department of Education (2002). Tests: Myths and realities. Testing for Results: Helping Families, Schools and Communities Understand and Improve Student Achievement.

Ysseldyke, J., Olsen, K. (1999). Putting Alternate Assessments into Practice: What To Measure and Possible Sources of Data, Exceptional Children, v65, 1999 ERIC #: ED416605.

WEBSITES

http://www.ed.gov/
Site offers research on aspects of inclusion, special education and assessment. Helpful information on Progress Monitoring and Curriculum Based Assessment.

http://education.umn.edu/nceo/TopicAreas/Accommodations/Accom_topic.htm
Site produced by National Center on Educational Outcomes with special topic areas including: accommodations, accountability and alternate assessments.

http://rubistar/4teachers.org
Site offers practical help in developing rubrics. A wide variety of rubrics are available for customizing. Sample rubrics paid for by federal funds for use by teachers.

http://education.umn.edu/NCEO/
Site offers insight into the construction of alternate assessments as well as the complexity and concerns related to their use.

http:// www.wrightslaw.com/
Resource that provides legal guidance in regard to special needs students.

TIPS-TIONARY FOR ASSESSMENT AND EVALUATION

1. **Alternate Assessment:** Alternate assessment is intended for targeted severely cognitively impaired special needs students in those situations when standard formal assessment is deemed inappropriate, even with accommodations.

   Pro: Allows for a more realistic tool to determine progress of special needs students.

   Con: NCLB limits the use of alternate assessment to only those students most significantly cognitively impaired. The IEP team, not the classroom teacher(s), determines student eligibility for this type of assessment. Alternate assessment is expected to relate to the general curriculum. No single model exists and there is much confusion and concern about appropriate construction.

2. **Alternative assessment:** Alternative assessment can include any manner of evaluating work or behavior such as observations, portfolios, demonstrations, presentations, rubrics, focus groups, subjective comments etc. Teachers may at one time or another use many different avenues for assessing student mastery and/or growth. Alternative assessment is not to be confused with *alternate assessment*.

   Pro: Offers a wide range of opportunities for students with diverse abilities. Offers insights not provided with traditional true/false, multiple-choice assessments.

   Con: Can be time consuming, may require intense teacher contact and support.

3. **Case studies:** In depth study and presentation of student/program needs, strengths, weaknesses as well as causative factors.

   Pro: Yields much information.
   Con: Can be subjective and time consuming.

4. **Contracts:** Teacher(s) and student(s) develop and agree to definite objectives, dates for check-in and completion as well as expectations for demonstrating mastery. Can be behavioral or academic and based upon needs or interest.

   Pro: Encourages independent growth. Allows for review, informal assessment and encouragement as student meets with teacher for check-in along the way to completion. Helpful for those special need students requiring growth toward independence yet in need of short-term reinforcement and support in completion of work.

   Con: For the busy teacher, requires the guidance and support of the teacher throughout the contract.

5. **Curriculum Based Assessment:** A tool for assessing content-based objectives such as rules, skills and procedures. Often professionally designed and associated with a given text.

   Pro: Helpful in assessing product and process but not progress unless done regularly. Often professionally prepared making administration and grading fairly easy. Better for rote evaluation than in-depth concept evaluation.

   Con: Often yields a 'small picture' of performance related to the overall curriculum.

6. **Focus group:** A group of selected students explores a topic in depth through study and discussion.

   Pro: Quick way to get impression of range and depth of understanding, can convey key information about learning, impressions, grasp of topic.

   Con: Requires objective and continual observation. Can get off course without structure.

7. **Functional behavioral assessment (FBA):** An assessment to determine the cause (or "function") of behavior before developing a program or intervention, particularly important when school districts are dealing with special needs students and serious discipline issues. The frequently used forms of assessment include interviews and rating scales and/or observation of the student's behavior. *(http://www.wrightslaw.com)*

8. **Group activity:** Students self-select work partners or are teacher assigned for a specific purpose. Work is to be completed within the group to fulfill given requirements. Students may be given multiple resources, multiple means of expression and presentation as well as multiple means of assessment.

    Pro: Allows for interpersonal development and acceptance of a variety of abilities. Can encourage individual growth toward responsible group effort. Can accommodate needs and skills of diverse learners.

    Con: Can be time consuming and difficult to assess individual vs. group contributions and to establish individual and group expectations. Objective individual assessment is difficult. Requires diligent teacher preparation, observation and guidance.

9. **Interview:** Teacher and students sit down and talk about how the student/teacher views progress, strengths and weaknesses. The student is encouraged to discuss alternative ways of accessing and demonstrating knowledge.

    Pro: Builds student/teacher bond and strengthens the notion of teamwork in learning.

    Con: Time consuming. Requires teacher to consider guidelines for discussion. Informal and subjective assessment. Will require tact and substantiation on part of teacher to offer constructive criticism.

10. **Letter or number grades:** Typical and widely used percentage grade or letters given to reflect level of performance or proficiency. Generally A, B, C, D, F, but sometimes E for excellence, G for good, F for fair, U for unsatisfactory.

    Pro: Quick. Often an expectation by students and parents.

    Con: Yields little critical information regarding strengths, deficits or progress. Subjective. Rewards able student. Does not identify areas for improvement.

11. **Narrative:** Teacher reviews student progress, product or process and then makes a written explanation and evaluation, preferably with substantiation to objectify comments.

    Pro: Gives personal response to work.

    Con: Subjective comments can be disputed unless specific criteria have been determined. Difficult to quantify and objectify without a rubric in place prior to the writing of the narrative.

12. **Objective assessment:** Involves aspects of preparation, delivery and presentation. A suitable rubric is best established prior to presentation.

    Pro: Establishes clear expectations and yields specific information about the level of mastery.

    Con: Not appropriate for reporting broad subject matter mastery.

13. **Observation:** Teacher routinely observes and notes student behaviors and/or performance.

    Pro: Informal, non-threatening. Can be ongoing. Efficient use of time. Helpful in continually aligning instruction to needs. Helpful in alerting teacher to skill or comprehension deficits in order to design intervention strategies.

    Con: Generally subjective.

14. **Pass/Fail:** Student either can or cannot respond correctly.

> **Pro:** Quick and easy.

> **Con:** Very general and can be misleading. Yields little constructive information about specific strengths or deficits. Can be discouraging to student who 'fails' and makes 'passing' student overconfident.

15. **Performance based assessment:** Teacher(s) develop(s) a scale to determine student progress or proficiency at completing a specific task or demonstrating knowledge. (Preferably developed with student input and with desired performance demonstrated prior to assessment.) Can be formal when the student knows that the assessment is taking place. Can be informal with teacher observing but student uninformed about it.

> **Pro:** Informal performance assessment can be a quick and easy way to determine level of student performance and determination of how much support is necessary. Good tool for poor traditional test-takers. Formal can be helpful in that both teacher(s) and student(s) benefit from specific information of performance level. Easily shared with parents.

> **Con:** Can be time consuming to determine criteria and to administer individually.

16. **Portfolios:** Portfolios are collections of student work over a period of time and representative of effort, progress and progress in a specific area. Portfolios materials can be teacher selected, student collected or collaboratively collected.

> **Pro:** Allows feedback to students and parents about strengths and deficits in relation to growth. Allows a value added approach to viewing a student's progress.

> **Con:** Time consuming. Should be a collection that is viewed in entirety. Requires storage space. Does not allow for precise measurement. Difficult for formal and objective assessment.

17. **Program evaluation:** Structured means of determining the quality of instruction and the extent to which academic and behavioral objectives (state, district, curricular, IEP, professional) are met.

> **Pro:** Allows professionals anxious to provide quality instruction to determine program successes and areas needing improvement.

> **Con:** Not required, time consuming, little training provided.

18. **Progress checklist:** Teacher(s) (possibly with student input) develop(s) a developmental ladder towards incremental progress. Teacher utilizes a commercially established checklist that corresponds to course objectives or behavioral goals. Teacher (and/or student) places a checkmark to indicate present level of performance/progress.

> **Pro:** Feedback to students and parents can be detailed and specific. Yields critical information regarding progress toward mastery as well as identifying deficiencies still to overcome.

> **Con:** Teacher (and student) must develop a baseline as a reference point from which to monitor growth. Essential to develop appropriate benchmarks or goal.

19. **Progress Monitoring:** The current level of performance is determined and student academic (or behavioral) performance is measured daily or weekly to track progress or lack of. Instructional materials and techniques are adjusted accordingly, sometimes used interchangeably (and not necessarily accurately) with Curricular Based Measurement or Assessment. The US Office of Special Education reminds us that it should be scientifically based and supported by significant research.

> **Pro:** The yield can be great for providing information for efficient and appropriate instruction, setting higher standards for teaching and learning and making more informed decisions.
>
> **Con:** Difficult for the untrained to implement without support.

20. **Quiz:** Short, formal or informal, oral or written, evaluation of specific subject matter. (Can be multiple choices; fill the blanks, true/false or short answer).

> **Pro:** Easily constructed. Allows for quick review of main ideas.
>
> **Con:** Yields superficial and sketchy view of mastery of specific subject matter.

21. **Rubric:** A rating scale or scoring guide devised to objectively measure student mastery on given topic or assignment. Rubrics can be developed by teacher(s) or in conjunction with students. Definite performance criteria are developed and shared prior to use. Holistic and analytic rubrics are used.

> **Pro:** Helps students work toward a higher standard by defining clear expectations, especially if students are co-authors of the rubric. Yields in-depth information for teacher, students and parents. Can be used across a variety of formats: individual or group work, written, visual, multi-media, etc.
>
> **Con:** Can be time consuming and difficult to construct and develop appropriate criteria that correspond with curricular objectives.

22. **Self-assessment:** Student assesses own process or product based upon pre-determined criteria. Student, teacher, or both may work to design rubric or checklist.

> **Pro:** Encourages student involvement and investment in assessment as a learning tool. Reduces student anxiety about assessment of performance or product while refocusing student on criteria for meeting predetermined standards.
>
> **Con:** Objectivity and reliability are questionable without a pre-set rubric.

23. **Student demonstrations or student taught lessons:** Student is given the opportunity to prepare and present a lesson on a selected (self or teacher-selected) topic. Demonstration may be multi-modal but should be toward pre-determined objectives.

> **Pro:** Risky but can be especially rewarding for the presenter.
> Student must really 'know' topic.
>
> **Con:** Time consuming. Teacher assistance required for all steps… researching, preparing, presenting and assessing quality of demonstration.

24. **Value Added Methods:** An attempt to revise current policies that hold teachers accountable for previous teacher/student failures whereby teachers accept students at varying academic levels and are expected to move them forward from that point to meet the current year's higher standards. The 'value added' method of assessment considers each student's entry level ability/performance at the start of the year. This is compared to exit level ability/performance at the conclusion of the year thereby determining the degree of 'value added.'